THRIFTY LIVING

*A Comprehensive Guide to Budgeting
and Living Well on a Dime.*

Millie Kiama

CONTENTS

OPENING REMARKS

Welcome to "Thrifty Living: A Comprehensive Guide to Budgeting and Living Well on a Dime." In the fast-paced world we live in, managing finances can be a daunting task. But fear not! This book is here to guide you through practical strategies, tips, and techniques to help you effectively manage your finances, stretch your dollars, and live a fulfilling life without breaking the bank.

In today's society, there's a common misconception that wealth and extravagance go hand in hand. However, if you take a closer look at many of the world's richest individuals, you'll find that they often embody a thrifty and frugal mindset. Contrary to popular belief, most rich people didn't amass their fortunes by squandering their wealth on lavish lifestyles. Instead, they understand the value of every dollar and prioritize smart spending and saving habits.

Consider some of the world's most successful entrepreneurs and investors. From Warren Buffett to Mark Zuckerberg, these individuals are known for their frugal habits and simple lifestyles. Despite their immense wealth, they live well below their means, opting for modest homes, driving economical cars, and avoiding unnecessary extravagances. By embracing frugality, they're able to maximize their savings, invest wisely, and build lasting wealth.

So why are most rich people thrifty and frugal? It's because they understand that financial success isn't about how much money you make—it's about how you manage and grow your wealth over time. By living below their means and prioritizing smart financial decisions, they're able to accumulate wealth steadily and sustainably.

In "Thrifty Living," we'll explore the principles and practices that have helped countless individuals achieve financial freedom and prosperity. From setting clear financial goals to cutting costs on everyday expenses to investing wisely for the future, this book will provide you with the tools and knowledge you need to take control of your finances and build a secure financial future.

So whether you're striving to pay off debt, save for a major purchase, or simply live more intentionally and sustainably, "Thrifty Living" is your roadmap to mastering the art of budgeting and living well on a dime. Let's embark on this journey together and discover the power of thrifty living to transform your financial life for the better.

* * *

CHAPTER1: UNDERSTANDING BUDGETING

B udgeting is not just about restricting yourself from spending—it's about empowering yourself to make smart financial decisions that align with your goals and values. In this chapter, we'll explore the significance of budgeting and equip you with practical strategies to create a budget that suits your lifestyle and aspirations.

Financial Stability: The Foundation of Budgeting

Imagine your finances as a ship navigating through the vast ocean of life. Without a clear direction or a steady hand at the helm, it's easy to drift aimlessly or even run aground. Budgeting serves as your navigational chart, guiding you towards financial stability and security. By setting sail with a well-crafted budget, you gain control over your finances and chart a course towards your desired destination.

Empowerment Through Knowledge

Budgeting is not about blindly restricting your spending—it's about understanding where your money goes and making intentional choices that align with your priorities. Take Sarah, for example. Faced with mounting expenses and a dwindling savings account, she decided to take control of her finances by tracking her expenses for a month. What she discovered was eye-opening: she was overspending on dining out and impulse purchases, draining her resources without realizing it. Armed with this newfound awareness, Sarah was able to reallocate her funds towards her savings goals and make more conscious spending decisions.

Creating Your Budget Blueprint

Creating a budget that works for you starts with setting clear goals and identifying your priorities. Whether you're saving for a dream vacation, paying off debt, or building an emergency fund, your budget should reflect your unique financial circumstances and aspirations. In this chapter, we'll provide you with practical tips and tools to help you craft a budget blueprint that suits your needs.

Tracking Your Expenses: The First Step Towards Financial Clarity

The cornerstone of any effective budgeting strategy is tracking your expenses. By keeping a record of every dollar you spend, you gain valuable insights into your spending habits and patterns. Whether you prefer to use a spreadsheet, a budgeting app, or pen and paper, the key is consistency. By diligently tracking your expenses, you'll be able to identify areas where you're overspending and make adjustments accordingly.

Identifying Areas for Savings: Making Every Dollar Count

Once you have a clear picture of your spending habits, it's time to identify areas where you can cut back and save money. From dining out less frequently to reducing impulse purchases to renegotiating your monthly bills, there are numerous opportunities to trim expenses and reallocate your funds towards your savings goals. In this chapter, we'll explore practical tips and strategies to help you make every dollar count and achieve your financial objectives.

In conclusion, understanding budgeting is the first step towards financial empowerment and security. By taking control of your finances, tracking your expenses, and making intentional spending decisions, you can create a budget that not only meets your needs but also helps you achieve your long-term financial goals. So let's embark on this journey together and discover the power of budgeting to transform your financial future.

❊ ❊ ❊

CHAPTER 2: ESSENTIAL MONEY-SAVING TIPS

I n our daily lives, we encounter a multitude of expenses, from groceries to household products, that can quickly deplete our wallets if not managed wisely. In this chapter, we will delve into essential money-saving tips to help you reduce your expenses without compromising on quality or convenience.

The Grocery Dilemma: Maximizing Value While Minimizing Costs

One of the most significant expenses for many households is groceries. However, with strategic planning and mindful shopping, you can stretch your food budget further than you ever thought possible. Take Mark, for example. Faced with rising grocery costs, he decided to take control of his spending by implementing several money-saving strategies. First, he started planning his meals for the week ahead, taking into account ingredients he already had on hand and incorporating affordable staples like beans, rice, and vegetables. By creating a shopping list based on his meal plan and sticking to it religiously, Mark avoided impulse purchases and stayed within his budget.

Utilizing Coupons and Discounts: Unlocking Hidden Savings

Coupons and discounts can be powerful tools for saving money on groceries and household essentials. With a bit of time and effort, you can uncover significant savings on items you purchase regularly. Mark discovered the value of couponing and began scouring newspapers, websites, and mobile apps for discounts on his favorite products. By combining coupons with store sales and promotions, he was able to maximize his savings and stretch his grocery budget even further.

Cooking at Home: The Key to Affordable and Nutritious Meals

Eating out can be convenient, but it often comes with a hefty price tag. By cooking at home and preparing meals from scratch, you not only save money but also have greater control over the ingredients and nutritional content of your food. Mark embraced home cooking as a way to save money and improve his health. He started experimenting with new recipes and cooking techniques, gradually building up his culinary skills and repertoire. By cooking in bulk and freezing leftovers for future meals, he was able to reduce food waste and lower his overall grocery expenses.

DIY Household Products: Savings Beyond the Grocery Aisle

In addition to groceries, household products such as cleaning supplies, toiletries, and personal care items can also take a toll on your budget. However, with a little creativity and resourcefulness, you can make many of these products at home for a fraction of the cost of store-bought alternatives. Mark began making his own cleaning solutions using simple ingredients like vinegar, baking soda, and essential oils. Not only were these homemade products more affordable, but they were also free from harsh chemicals and toxins, making them better for his health and the environment.

In conclusion, mastering essential money-saving tips is key to achieving financial freedom and security. By implementing strategies such as meal planning, couponing, cooking at home, and making DIY household products, you can significantly reduce your expenses and free up more money for the things that matter most to you. So let's embrace these money-saving tips and embark on a journey towards a more frugal, yet fulfilling, lifestyle.

CHAPTER 3: FRUGAL LIVING STRATEGIES

I n every facet of our lives, there are ample opportunities to adopt frugal living strategies that not only help us minimize expenses but also maximize savings. From transportation to housing to entertainment, embracing a frugal mindset can lead to significant financial benefits. In this chapter, we will explore various frugal living strategies to empower you to take control of your spending and achieve your financial goals.

Maximizing Savings on Transportation

Transportation expenses can quickly add up, but with a bit of creativity and planning, you can significantly reduce your costs. Take Emily, for example. Faced with high fuel prices and mounting car maintenance expenses, she decided to explore alternative modes of transportation. By carpooling with coworkers, biking to nearby destinations, and utilizing public transportation whenever feasible, Emily was able to slash her transportation costs dramatically. Moreover, she opted for a fuel-efficient vehicle and minimized unnecessary car trips, further contributing to her savings. By embracing these frugal transportation strategies, Emily not only saved hundreds of dollars each month but also reduced her environmental footprint.

Housing Hacks for Financial Freedom

Housing expenses often represent a significant portion of our monthly budget, but there are numerous ways to minimize these costs without sacrificing comfort or convenience. Whether you're renting or owning, there are several frugal living strategies you can employ to save money on housing. For renters, consider downsizing to a smaller apartment, negotiating lower rent with your landlord, or exploring shared living arrangements to split costs. For homeowners, refinancing your mortgage, renting out spare rooms, or taking advantage of energy-saving upgrades can help reduce expenses over the long term. By adopting these frugal housing hacks, you can free up more money for savings or other financial priorities.

Energy-Saving Tips for Lower Utility Bills

Utility bills, including electricity, water, and gas, can eat into your budget if left unchecked. However, by implementing energy-saving tips and making simple changes to your habits and lifestyle, you can lower your utility bills and save money each month. Start by investing in energy-efficient appliances, installing programmable thermostats, and sealing drafts to improve your home's energy efficiency. Additionally, practice water conservation by fixing leaks, taking shorter showers, and using water-saving fixtures. By being mindful of your energy and water usage, you can significantly reduce your utility bills and contribute to a more sustainable future.

Cutting Costs on Entertainment and Leisure Activities

Entertainment and leisure activities are essential for relaxation and enjoyment, but they can also be a source of significant expenses. Fortunately, there are numerous frugal living strategies you can employ to enjoy entertainment without breaking the bank. Instead of dining out at expensive restaurants, consider hosting potluck dinners with friends or enjoying picnics in the park. Explore free or low-cost entertainment options such as outdoor concerts, movie nights at home, or hiking and biking trails. By getting creative and thinking outside the box, you can have fun while saving money on entertainment and leisure activities.

In conclusion, adopting frugal living strategies can lead to significant financial benefits and empower you to achieve your long-term financial goals. Whether it's maximizing savings on transportation, minimizing housing expenses, reducing utility bills, or cutting costs on entertainment, there are numerous opportunities to live frugally without sacrificing quality of life. By embracing these frugal living strategies, you can take control of your finances, build a secure future, and live a fulfilling life within your means.

CHAPTER 4: DEBT MANAGEMENT AND SAVINGS

D ebt can cast a long shadow over your financial well-being, but with careful planning and disciplined strategies, you can overcome this burden and pave the way towards a debt-free future. In this chapter, we will delve into practical debt management strategies and explore how to simultaneously build an emergency fund and plan for long-term savings and retirement. Drawing inspiration from John's success story, we'll uncover actionable steps to help you take control of your finances and achieve financial freedom.

Understanding Debt: Breaking Free from the Cycle

Before diving into debt management strategies, it's essential to understand the different types of debt and how they impact your financial health. From credit card debt to student loans to mortgages, debt comes in various forms, each with its own set of challenges and considerations. By assessing your current debt situation and understanding the terms and interest rates associated with each debt, you can develop a tailored debt repayment plan that aligns with your financial goals.

Paying Off Debt: Strategies for Success

Paying off debt requires a combination of discipline, focus, and strategic planning. One effective approach is the debt avalanche method, where you prioritize paying off debts with the highest interest rates first while making minimum payments on other debts. This method allows you to minimize interest charges and pay off debt more quickly. Alternatively, you may opt for the debt snowball method, where you focus on paying off debts with the smallest balances first to gain momentum and motivation. Whichever approach you choose, the key is to stay consistent and committed to your debt repayment plan.

Building an Emergency Fund: Financial Security for the Unexpected

While paying off debt is crucial, it's equally important to build an emergency fund to protect yourself from unexpected expenses or financial emergencies. An emergency fund serves as a safety net, allowing you to cover unexpected costs without resorting to additional debt. Aim to save at least three to six months' worth of living expenses in an easily accessible savings account. Start small by setting aside a portion of your income each month and gradually increase your savings over time. By prioritizing both debt repayment and emergency fund savings, you can achieve greater financial security and peace of mind.

Planning for Long-Term Savings and Retirement

In addition to paying off debt and building an emergency fund, it's essential to prioritize long-term savings and retirement planning. Take advantage of employer-sponsored retirement plans such as 401(k)s or IRAs, and contribute enough to receive any employer matching contributions. Aim to save at least 10-15% of your income towards retirement each year, adjusting your contributions as your financial situation evolves. Automate your savings contributions to ensure consistency and discipline, and regularly review your investment portfolio to ensure it aligns with your long-term goals and risk tolerance.

In conclusion, debt management and savings are critical components of financial health and well-being. By developing a structured debt repayment plan, building an emergency fund, and prioritizing long-term savings and retirement planning, you can take control of your finances and work towards a brighter financial future. Remember, consistency, discipline, and patience are key to achieving financial freedom. With determination and perseverance, you can break free from the cycle of debt and build a secure foundation for a prosperous life ahead.

CHAPTER 5: THRIFTY LIFESTYLE CHOICES

L iving a thrifty lifestyle goes beyond mere frugality—it's about embracing a mindset of simplicity, sustainability, and mindful consumption. In this chapter, we will explore thrifty lifestyle choices that can help you live more intentionally, reduce waste, and find greater satisfaction and fulfillment in your everyday life. Drawing inspiration from Lisa's journey towards minimalism, we'll uncover practical tips and strategies to help you prioritize experiences over material possessions and cultivate a "less is more" mindset.

Embracing Minimalism: Finding Joy in Simplicity

At its core, minimalism is about decluttering your life—both physically and mentally—and focusing on what truly matters. By reducing the number of possessions you own and simplifying your surroundings, you can create space for greater clarity, peace, and fulfillment. Take a cue from Lisa, who embarked on a journey towards minimalism by decluttering her home and letting go of items that no longer served her. By paring down her possessions to the essentials and surrounding herself only with things that brought her joy, she discovered a newfound sense of freedom and contentment.

Prioritizing Experiences Over Material Possessions

In a world that often equates success and happiness with material wealth and possessions, it's easy to lose sight of what truly brings us joy and fulfillment. Instead of chasing after the latest gadgets or fashion trends, consider investing your time and resources in experiences that enrich your life and create lasting memories. Whether it's traveling to new destinations, exploring nature, or spending quality time with loved ones, prioritizing experiences over material possessions can lead to greater happiness and fulfillment. Follow Lisa's example by shifting your focus from acquiring things to savoring moments and building meaningful connections with others.

Cultivating a "Less is More" Mindset

In a culture that glorifies excess and consumerism, adopting a "less is more" mindset can be revolutionary. Instead of constantly seeking more, strive to find contentment and satisfaction in what you already have. By embracing simplicity and living within your means, you can reduce stress, increase gratitude, and live a more fulfilling life. Challenge yourself to resist the temptation of impulse purchases and unnecessary upgrades, and instead, focus on maximizing the value and utility of the things you already own. By cultivating a mindset of abundance and gratitude, you can find joy and fulfillment in the simple pleasures of everyday life.

In conclusion, living a thrifty lifestyle is about more than just cutting costs—it's about embracing simplicity, sustainability, and mindful consumption. By prioritizing experiences over material possessions, decluttering your life, and cultivating a "less is more" mindset, you can find greater satisfaction and fulfillment in every aspect of your life. So let's embark on this journey together and discover the joys of living intentionally and sustainably in a world that often values excess and extravagance.

CLOSING REMARKS

"Thrifty Living" serves as your comprehensive guide to mastering the art of budgeting and living well on a dime. Throughout this book, we have explored a variety of strategies, tips, and techniques to help you take control of your finances, minimize expenses, and maximize savings. From understanding the importance of budgeting to adopting frugal lifestyle choices, each chapter has provided valuable insights and practical advice to empower you on your journey towards financial freedom and fulfillment.

By implementing the strategies and tips outlined in this book, you can transform your relationship with money and experience greater peace of mind and security. Whether you're looking to pay off debt, build savings, or simply live more intentionally and sustainably, "Thrifty Living" offers a wealth of resources and guidance to help you achieve your goals.

So let's embark on this journey together and discover the joys of thrifty living! Whether you're a seasoned budgeting pro or just starting out on your financial journey, there's something for everyone in these pages. With determination, discipline, and a willingness to embrace change, you can take control of your finances and live a more fulfilling life—one penny at a time.

* * *

ABOUT THE AUTHOR

Millie Kiama

Millie Kiama, also known by her pen name Misty Miracle, is an accomplished author and avid reader with a rich background rooted in a small town in Kenya. Her formative years were spent immersed in the pages of both fictional and non-fictional books at her local library, igniting a fervent passion for storytelling. Enthralled by fiction's remarkable ability to transport readers to alternate realms, Millie embarked on a determined journey to become a writer herself.

Now residing in Keller, Texas, Millie not only crafts captivating stories across genres but also serves as a Resource teacher, dedicated to nurturing young minds and instilling within them a deep appreciation for literature and creative expression, particularly in the realm of fiction. Her dual roles as an author and educator reflect her unwavering commitment to fostering a love for reading and writing in others. Millie is also passionate about helping women and children to achieve their highest potential, and their issues are near and dear to her heart.

Her books can be easily found by searching for her titles by her name, Millie Kiama, or by her pen name Misty Miracle. Whether you're seeking inspiration, guidance, or entertainment, Millie's diverse range of publications offers something for every reader. So dive into her captivating narratives and embark on a journey of imagination and enlightenment.

Millie's trajectory from her modest beginnings to achieving her dreams stands as a powerful testament to the transformative force of imagination and perseverance. Through her work, she continues to inspire others to embrace the magic of storytelling and to embark on their own journeys of literary exploration and self-discovery.